Growing up

written by Jay Dale

Look at this new baby.
This baby has just been born.

When you were born,
you would have looked
just like this!

When you were just a little bit older,
you could rest on your tummy
and lift your head.

This baby can *crawl* and say, "Goo-ga!"
Did you say, "Goo-ga"
when you were a little baby?

This baby can smile and laugh.
She can hold her *bottle*, too.

5

1

This baby is one year old.
He can walk by himself,
and he likes to eat baby food!

Yum!

6

Lots of babies can say,
"Mumma", "Dadda" and "bubba".
What could you say when you were one?

2

This baby is called a *toddler*.

She is two years old.

She can jump up and down.

She can hold a *crayon* in her hand.

This little toddler can do lots of new things! What could you do when you were two?

3

This little boy is three years old.

Some children go to nursery when they are three.

This little boy can do lots of things.

He can make a *tower* with *blocks*.

He can do up his own *buttons*.

He can *talk* a lot, too!

Did you talk a lot

when you were three?

4

Lots of children go to nursery when they are four.
Children at nursery can *paint*.
They can hop on one leg, too.

They love to look at books
and play with their friends.
Did you play with your friends
when you were at nursery?

This little girl is five years old.
She has just started school.
There are lots and lots
of things she can do.
She can *skip*.
She can dress herself.
She has also just started to read!

Did you start to read
when you were five?

5

Now that you are older, what can **you** do?

Picture Glossary

skip

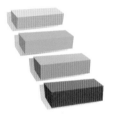
blocks

crawl

talk

bottle

crayon

toddler

buttons

paint

tower